ESSENTIAL ELEMENTS for Band

COMPREHENSIVE BAND METHOD

TIM LAUTZENHEISER • JOHN HIGGINS • CHARLES MENGHINI
PAUL LAVENDER • TOM C. RHODES • DON BIERSCHENK

These piano accompaniments can provide helpful guidance for teaching beginning instrumentalists. The format includes a cue line to provide the director or pianist with a visual guide of the student melody part.

The harmony and style of each piano example are fully compatible with the online audio accompaniment tracks included with each student book.

Each example also includes chord symbols for the director or pianist to adapt the written part as needed for specific teaching situations.

ISBN 979-835015515-0

HAL•LEONARD®
A Muse Group Company

Visit Hal Leonard Online at
www.halleonard.com

World headquarters, contact:
Hal Leonard
7777 West Bluemound Road
Milwaukee, WI 53213
Email: info@halleonard.com

In Europe, contact:
Hal Leonard Europe Limited
1 Red Place
London, W1K 6PL
Email: info@halleonardeurope.com

In Australia, contact:
Hal Leonard Australia Pty. Ltd.
4 Lentara Court
Cheltenham, Victoria, 3192 Australia
Email: info@halleonard.com.au

1. THE FIRST NOTE

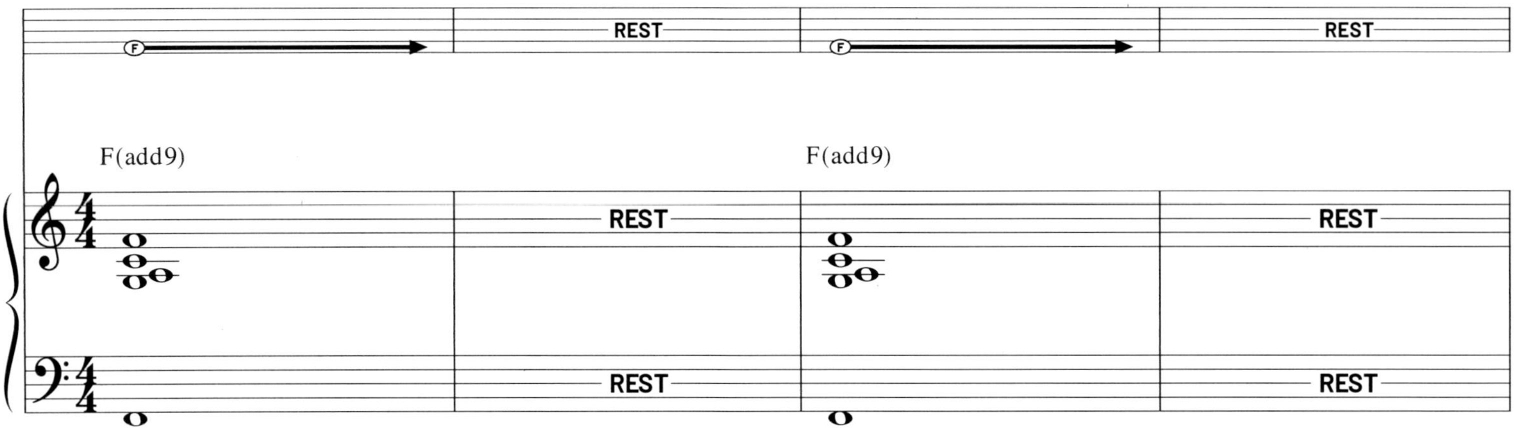

2. COUNT AND PLAY

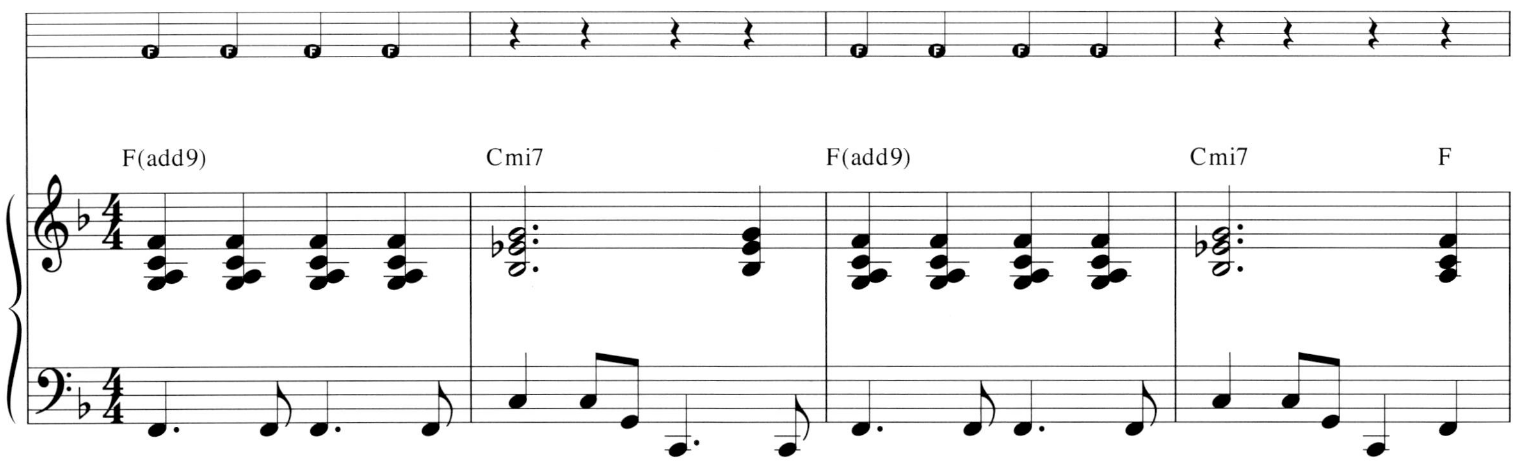

3. A NEW NOTE

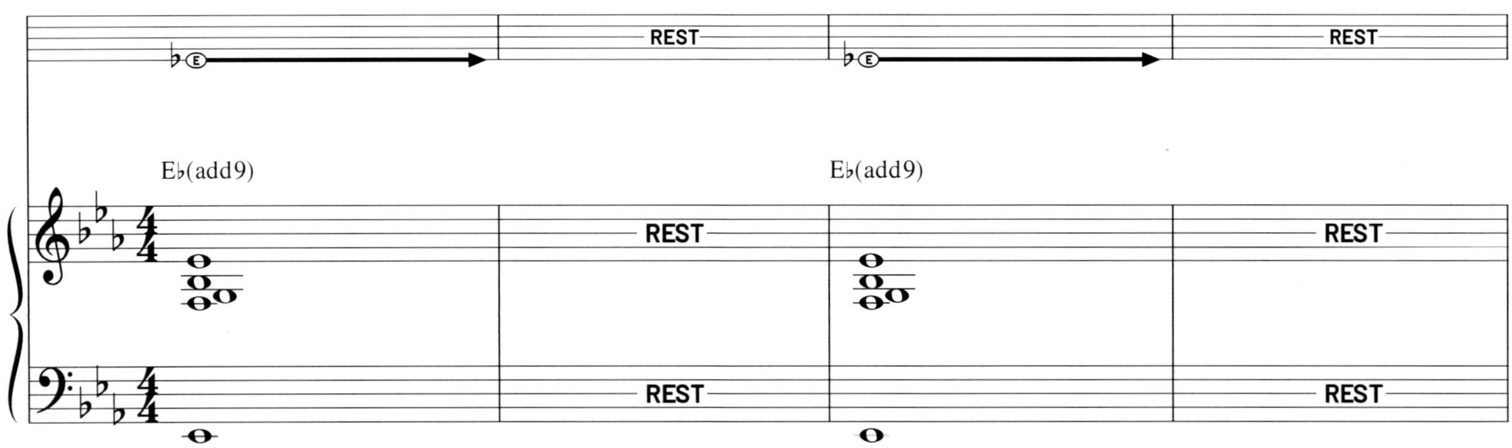

4. TWO'S A TEAM

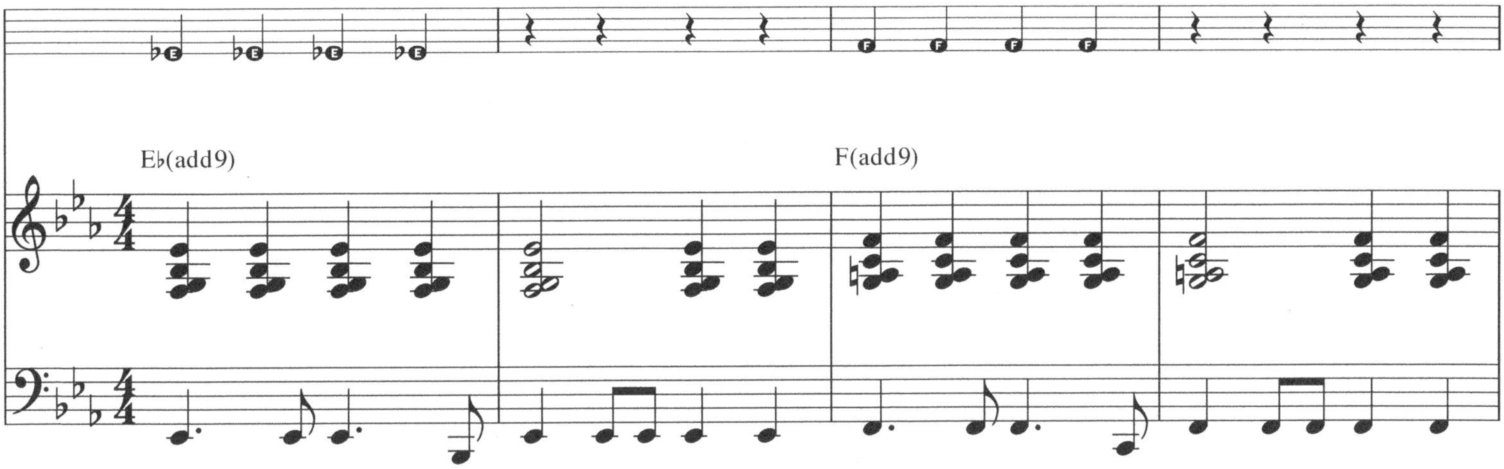

5. HEADING DOWN

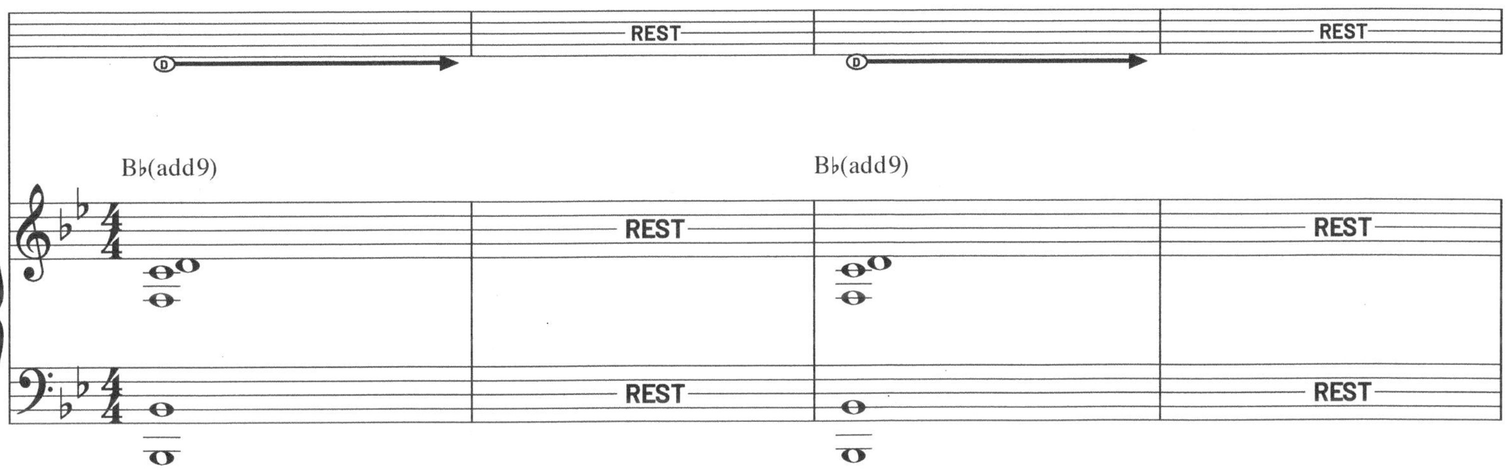

6. MOVING ON UP

7. THE LONG HAUL

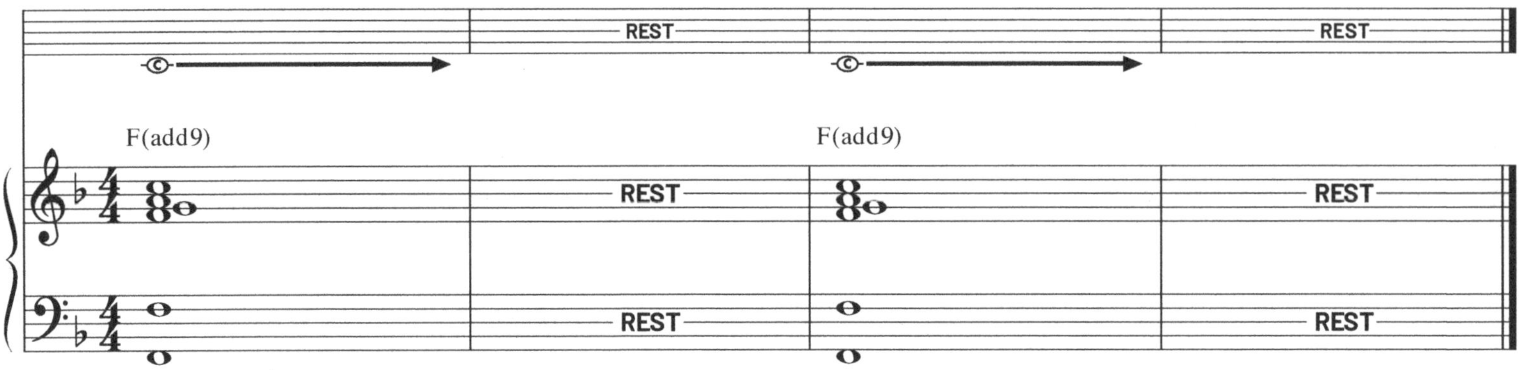

8. FOUR BY FOUR

Student books have repeats, not 1st and 2nd endings (until ex. 76).

9. TOUCHDOWN

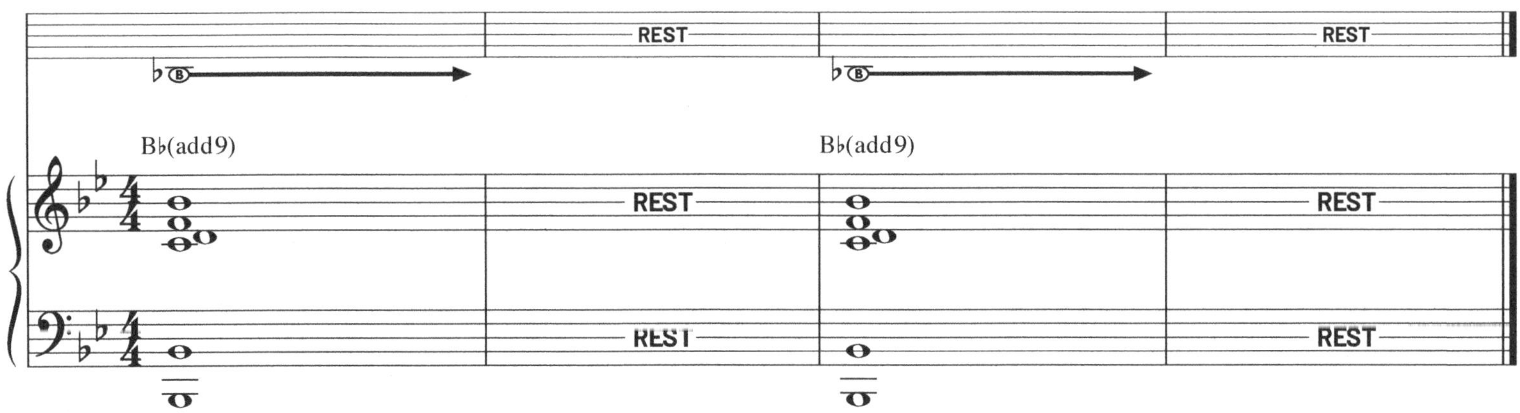

10. THE FAB FIVE

11. READING THE NOTES

12. FIRST FLIGHT

13. ESSENTIAL ELEMENTS QUIZ

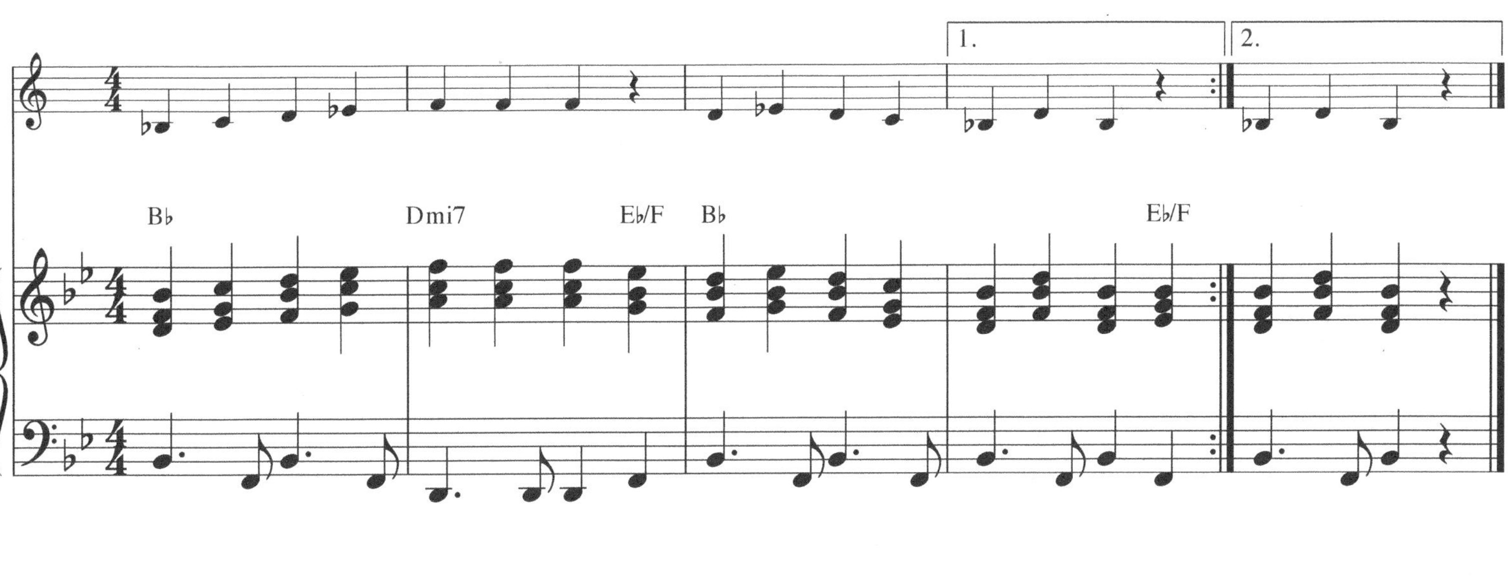

14. ROLLING ALONG

15. RHYTHM RAP

16. THE HALF COUNTS

17. HOT CROSS BUNS

18. GO TELL AUNT RHODIE

American Folk Song

19. ESSENTIAL ELEMENTS QUIZ

20. RHYTHM RAP

21. THE WHOLE THING

22. SPLIT DECISION – Duet

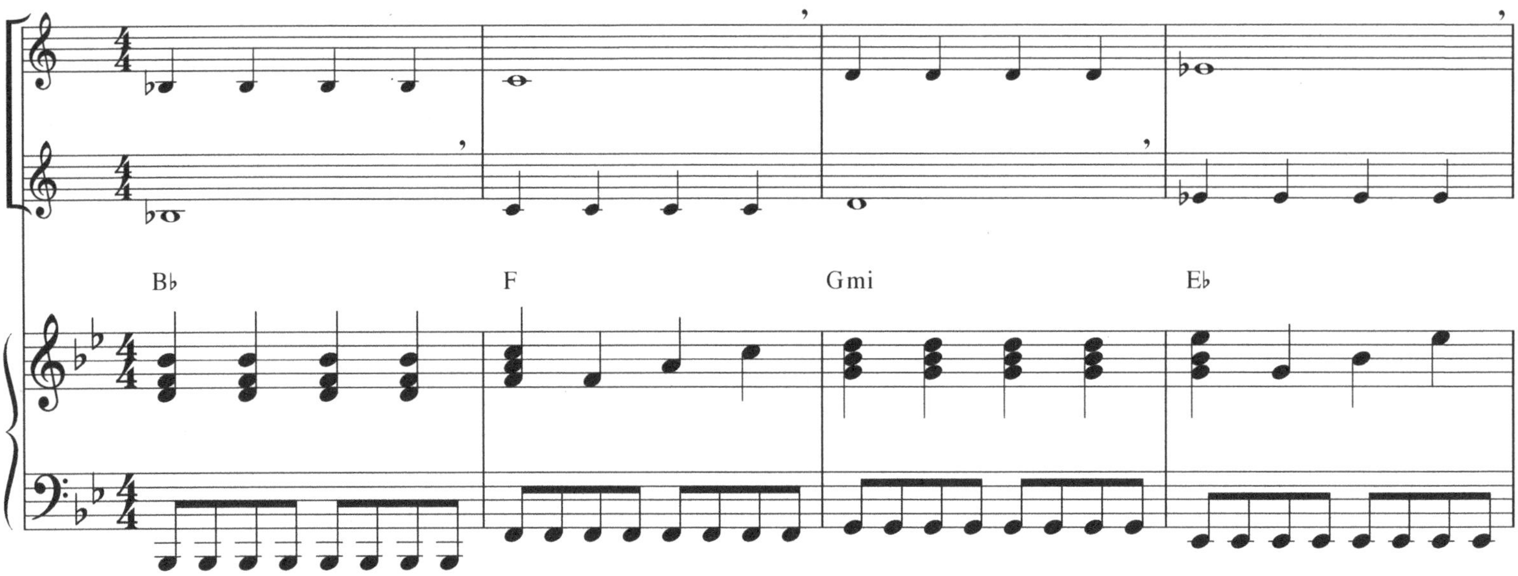

23. MARCH STEPS

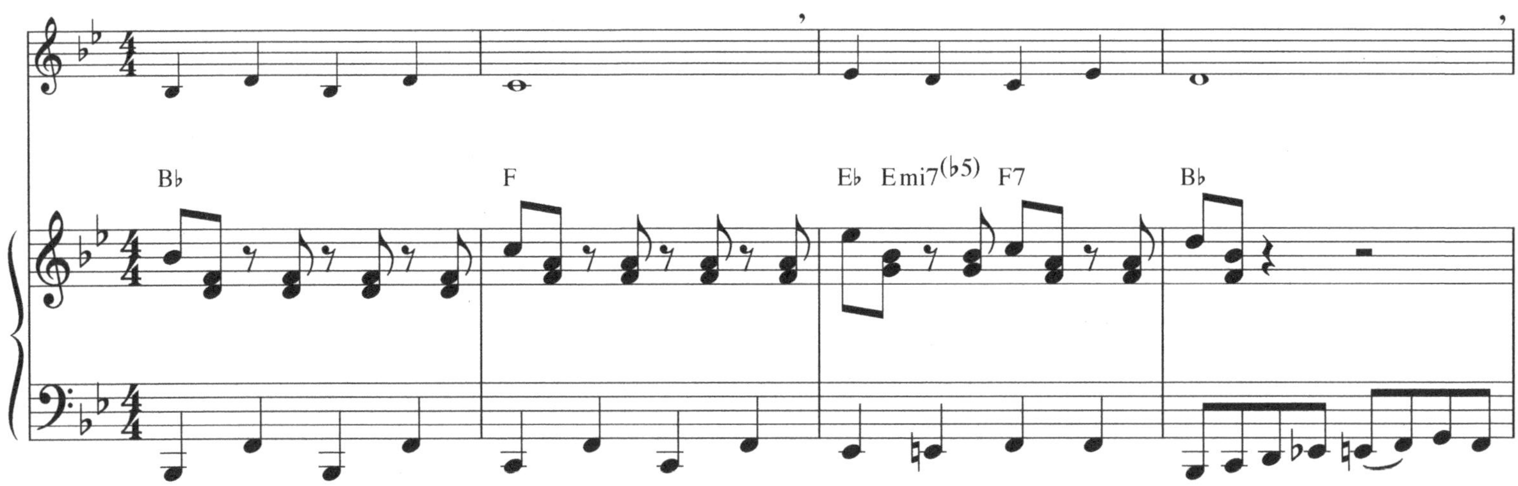

24. LISTEN TO OUR SECTIONS

25. LIGHTLY ROW

26. ESSENTIAL ELEMENTS QUIZ

27. REACHING HIGHER

28. AU CLAIRE DE LA LUNE

French Folk Song

29. REMIX

30. LONDON BRIDGE – Duet

English Folk Song

31. A MOZART MELODY

Adaptation

32. ESSENTIAL ELEMENTS QUIZ

33. DEEP POCKETS

34. DOODLE ALL DAY

35. JUMP ROPE

36. A-TISKET, A-TASKET

37. LOUD AND SOFT

38. JINGLE BELLS

J. S. Pierpont

39. MY DREYDL

Traditional Hanukkah Song

Student Book Page 10

40. RHYTHM RAP

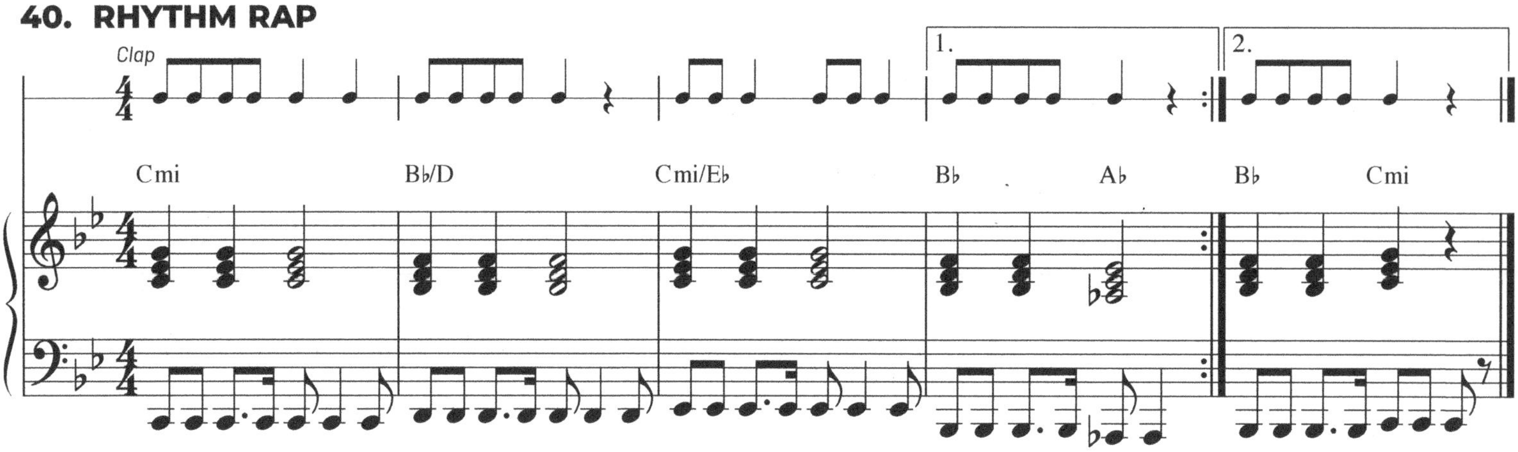

41. EIGHTH NOTE JAM

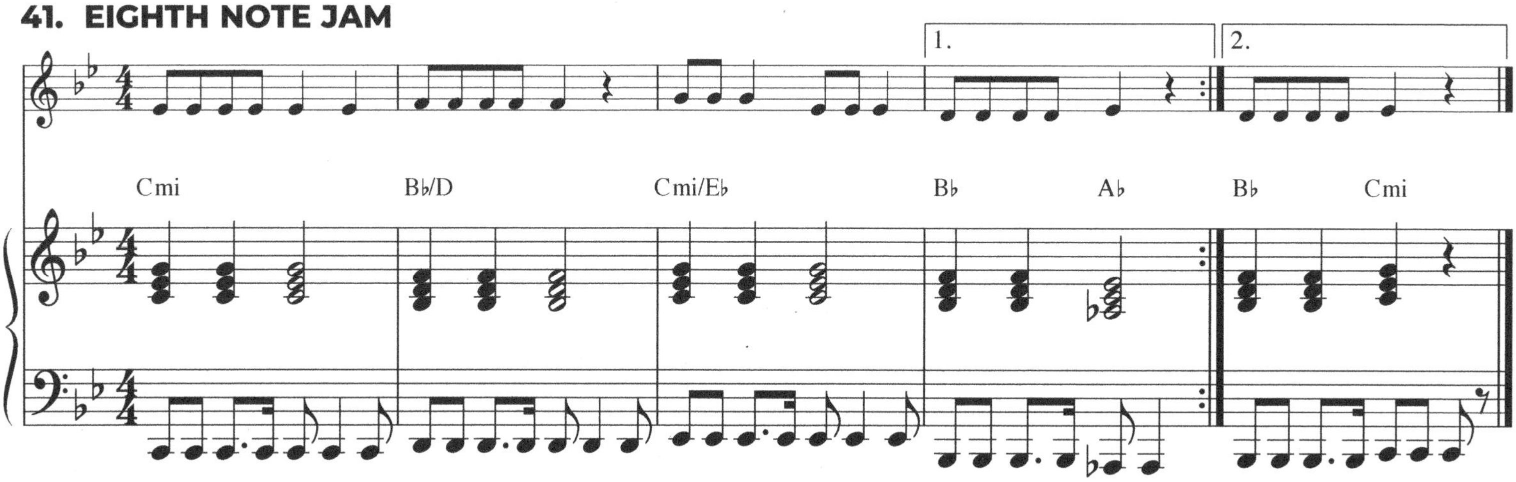

42. SKIP TO MY LOU

American Folk Song

43. LONG, LONG AGO

44. CANDY MOUNTAIN ROCK

45. ESSENTIAL ELEMENTS QUIZ — WILLIAM TELL

Gioachino Rossini

46. RHYTHM RAP

47. TWO BY TWO

48. HIGH SCHOOL CADETS – March

John Philip Sousa

Allegro

49. HEY, HO! NOBODY'S HOME

Moderato

50. CLAP THE DYNAMICS

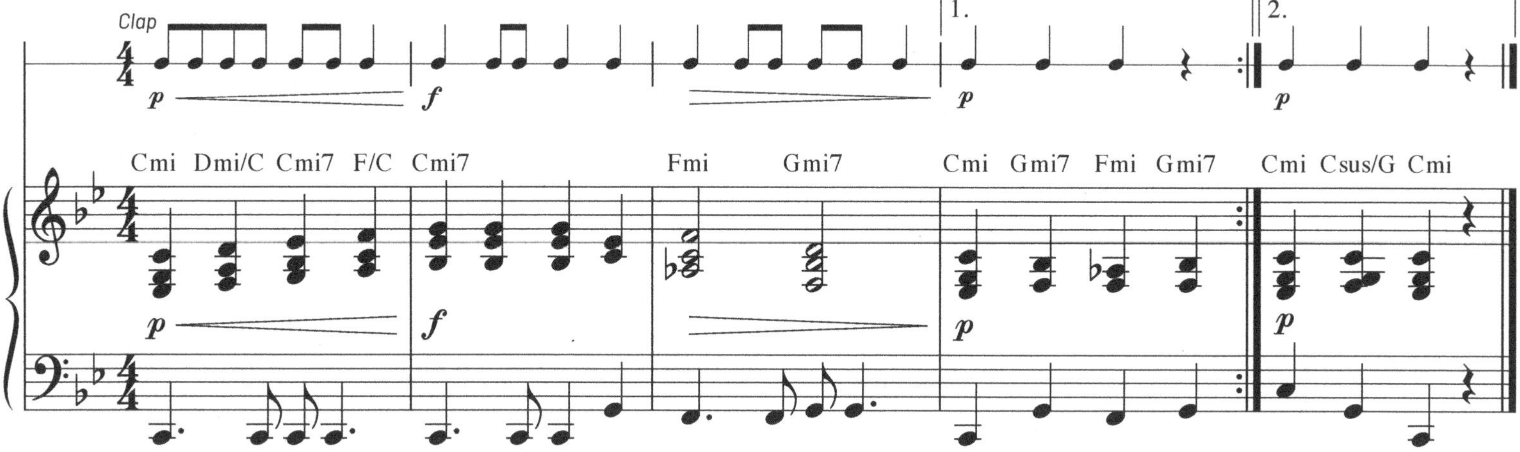

51. PLAY THE DYNAMICS

52. PERFORMANCE WARM-UPS

TONE BUILDER

RHYTHM ETUDE

RHYTHM RAP

CHORALE

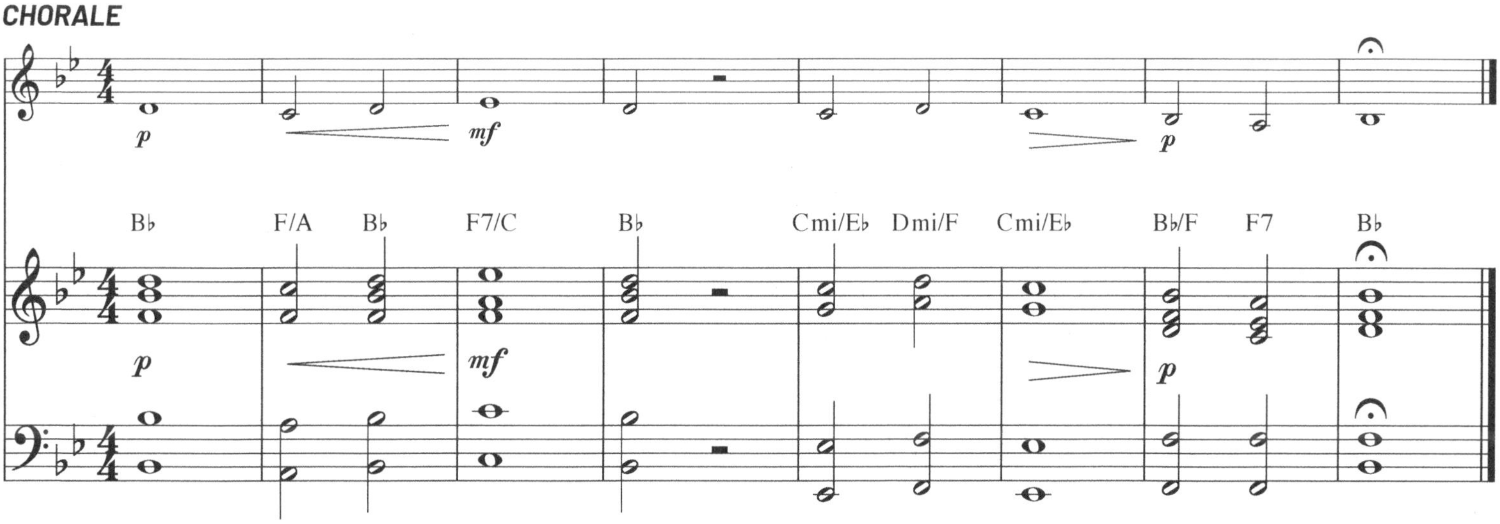

53. AURA LEE – Duet or Band Arrangement

George R. Poulton

54. FRÈRE JACQUES – Round *(When group A reaches ② group B begins at ①)*

55. WHEN THE SAINTS GO MARCHING IN – Band Arrangement

Arr. by John Higgins

56. OLD MACDONALD HAD A BAND – Section Feature

57. ODE TO JOY (from Symphony No. 9)

Ludwig van Beethoven
Arr. by John Higgins

58. HARD ROCK BLUES – Encore

John Higgins

59. FIT TO BE TIED

60. ALOUETTE

French-Canadian Folk Song

61. ALOUETTE – THE SEQUEL

French-Canadian Folk Song

62. IT'S RAINING

Student Book Page 14

63. NEW DIRECTIONS

64. THE NOBLES

65. ESSENTIAL ELEMENTS QUIZ

66. RHYTHM RAP

67. THREE BEAT JAM

68. BARCAROLLE

Moderato

Jacques Offenbach

69. MORNING (from Peer Gynt)

Edvard Grieg

70. ACCENT YOUR TALENT

71. MEXICAN CLAPPING SONG ("Chiapanecas")

Latin American Folk Song

72. ESSENTIAL CREATIVITY – *Writing assignment in student books.*

73. HOT MUFFINS

74. COSSACK DANCE

75. BASIC BLUES

76. HIGH FLYING

77. SAKURA, SAKURA – Band Arrangement

Japanese Folk Song
Arr. by John Higgins

78. UP ON A HOUSETOP

79. JOLLY OLD ST. NICK – Duet

Moderato

80. THE BIG AIRSTREAM

81. WALTZ THEME

Franz Lehar

82. AIR TIME

83. DOWN BY THE STATION

84. ESSENTIAL ELEMENTS QUIZ

85. ESSENTIAL CREATIVITY *Using these notes, improvise your own rhythms:*

86. TONE BUILDER

87. RHYTHM BUILDER

Student books have repeats, not 1st and 2nd endings.

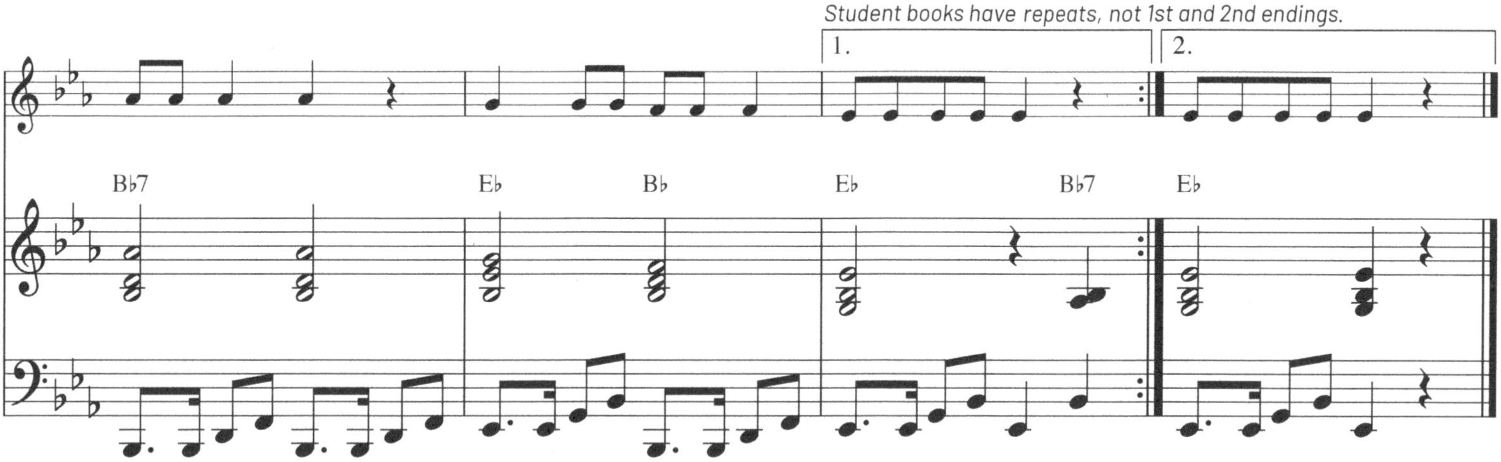

88. TECHNIQUE TRAX

Student books have repeats, not 1st and 2nd endings.

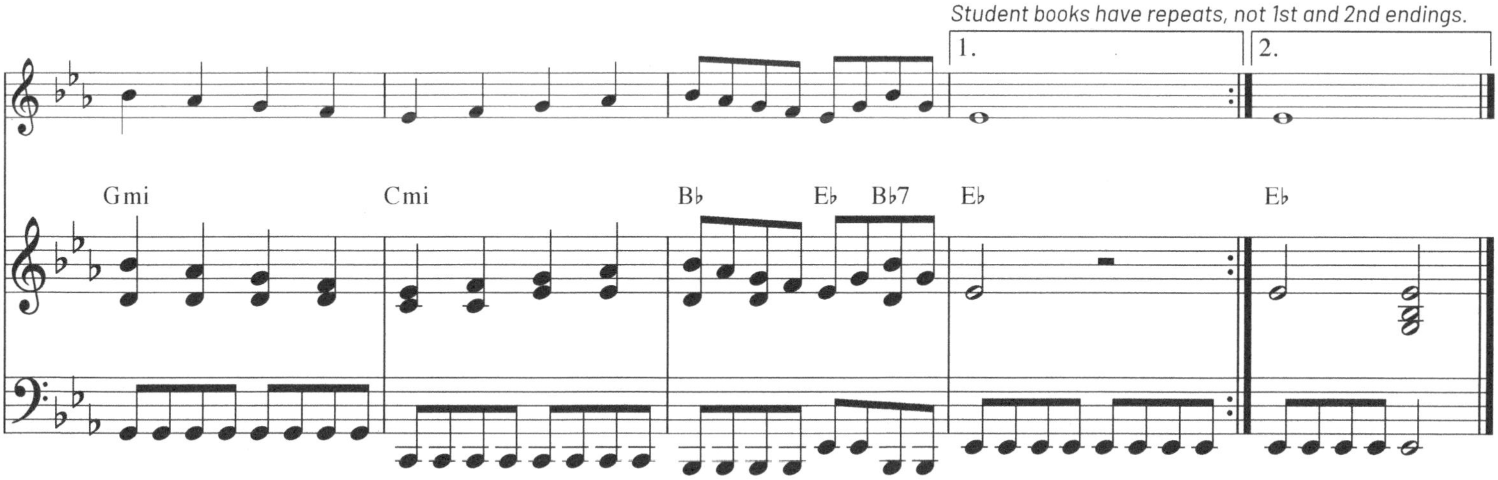

89. CHORALE *(Adapted from Cantata 147)*

Johann Sebastian Bach

90. VARIATIONS ON A FAMILIAR THEME

91. BANANA BOAT SONG

Caribbean Folk Song

Student Book Page 19

92. RAZOR'S EDGE

93. THE MUSIC BOX

94. EZEKIEL SAW THE WHEEL

African-American Spiritual

95. SMOOTH OPERATOR

96. GLIDING ALONG

97. TROMBONE RAG

98. ESSENTIAL ELEMENTS QUIZ

Student books have a D.C. al Fine at measure 8 with the Fine at measure 4.

99. TAKE THE LEAD

100. THE COLD WIND

101. PHRASEOLOGY

102. SATIN LATIN

103. MINUET – Duet

Johann Sebastian Bach

104. ESSENTIAL CREATIVITY – *Writing assignment in student books.*

105. NATURALLY

106. MARCH MILITAIRE

Allegro

Franz Schubert

107. THE FLAT ZONE

108. ON TOP OF OLD SMOKEY

American Folk Song

109. BOTTOM BASS BOOGIE – Duet

110. RHYTHM RAP

111. THE DOT ALWAYS COUNTS

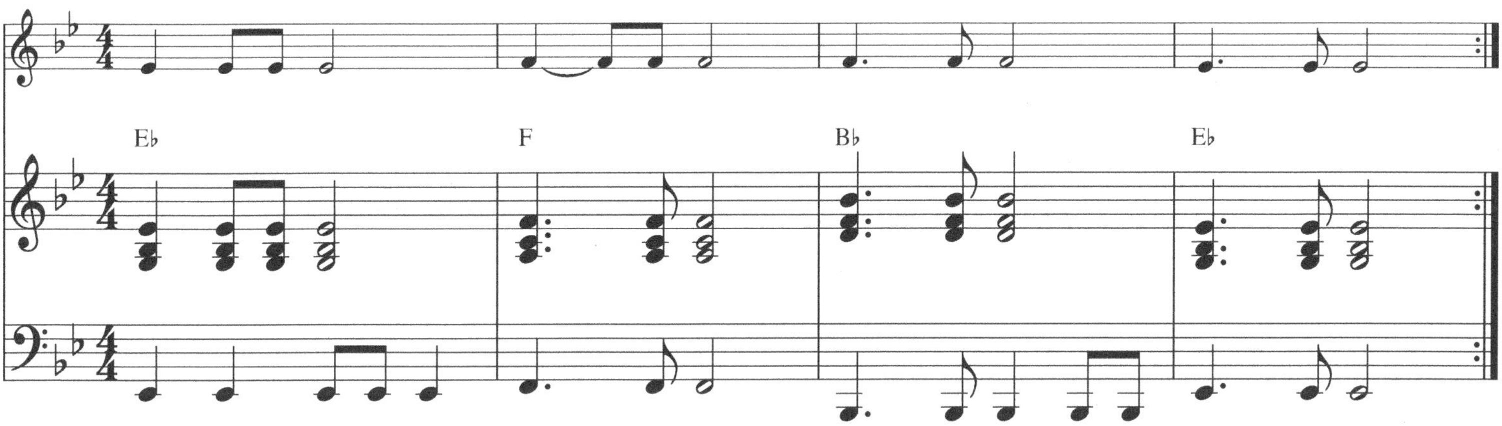

112. ALL THROUGH THE NIGHT

113. SEA CHANTY

English Folk Song

114. SCARBOROUGH FAIR

English Folk Song

115. RHYTHM RAP

116. THE TURNAROUND

117. ESSENTIAL ELEMENTS QUIZ – AULD LANG SYNE

Scottish Folk Song

118. THEME FROM "NEW WORLD SYMPHONY"

Antonin Dvorák

119. GRENADILLA GORILLA JUMP No. 1

120. JUMPIN' UP AND DOWN

121. GRENADILLA GORILLA JUMP No. 2

122. JUMPIN' FOR JOY

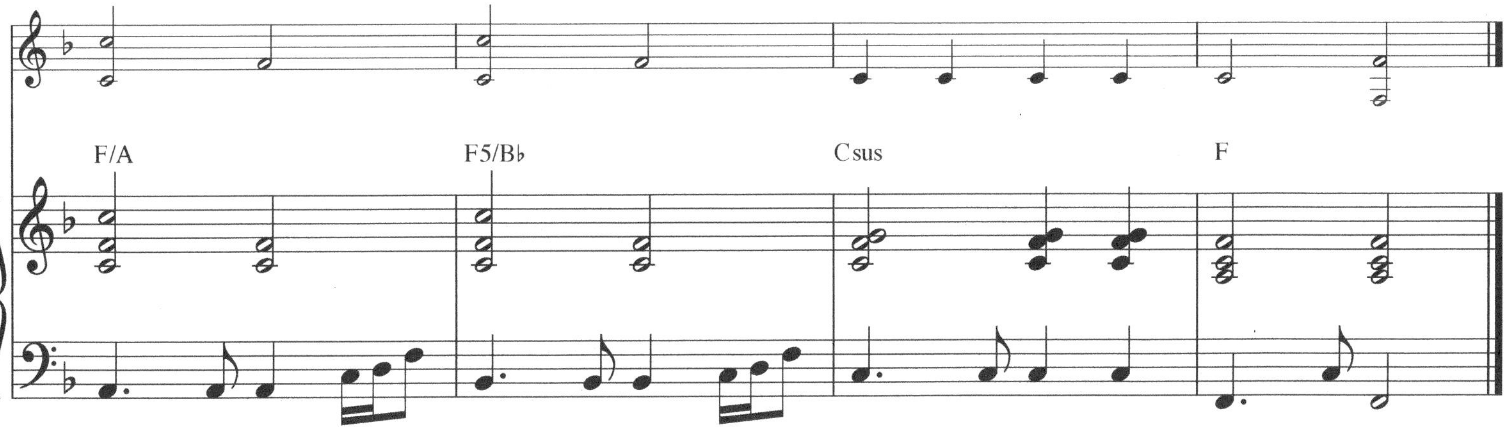

123. GRENADILLA GORILLA JUMP No. 3

124. JUMPIN' JACKS

125. ESSENTIAL ELEMENTS QUIZ

126. GRENADILLA GORILLA JUMP No. 4

127. THREE IS THE COUNT

128. GRENADILLA GORILLA JUMP No. 5

129. TECHNIQUE TRAX

130. CROSSING OVER

131. KUM BAH YAH – Trio

African Folk Song

132. MICHAEL ROW THE BOAT ASHORE

African-American Spiritual

133. AUSTRIAN WALTZ

Austrian Folk Song

Student books have repeats, not 1st and 2nd endings.

134. BOTANY BAY

Australian Folk Song

135. TECHNIQUE TRAX

Student books have repeats, not 1st and 2nd endings.

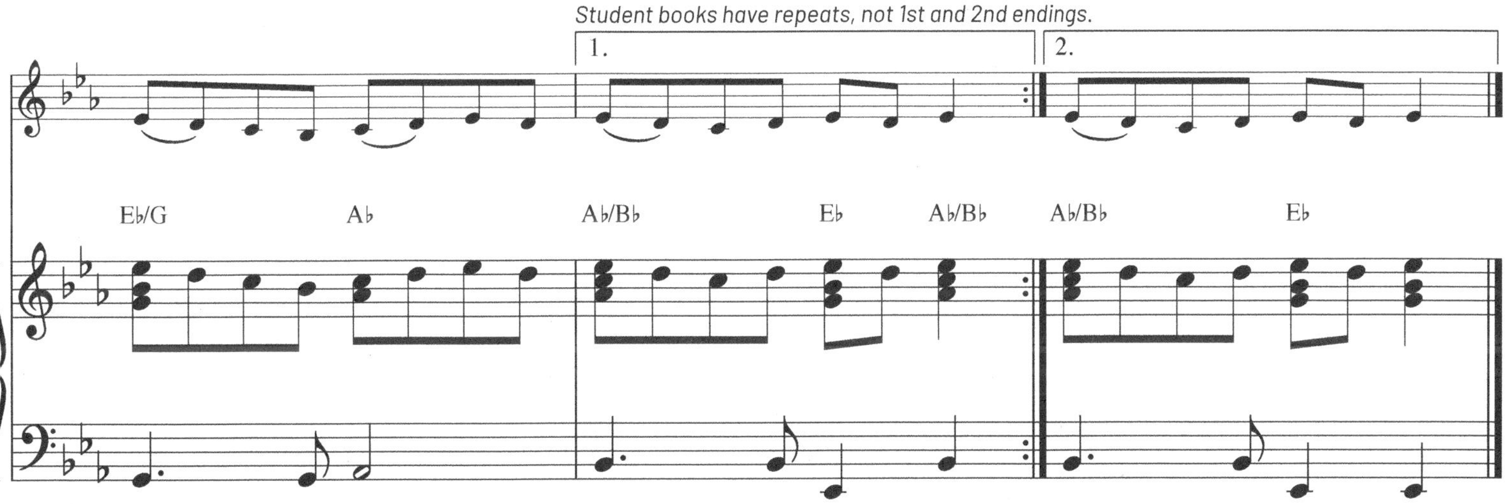

136. FINLANDIA

Jean Sibelius

137. ESSENTIAL CREATIVITY

Create your own variations by penciling in a dot and a flag to change the rhythm of any measure from ♩ ♩ *to* ♩. ♪

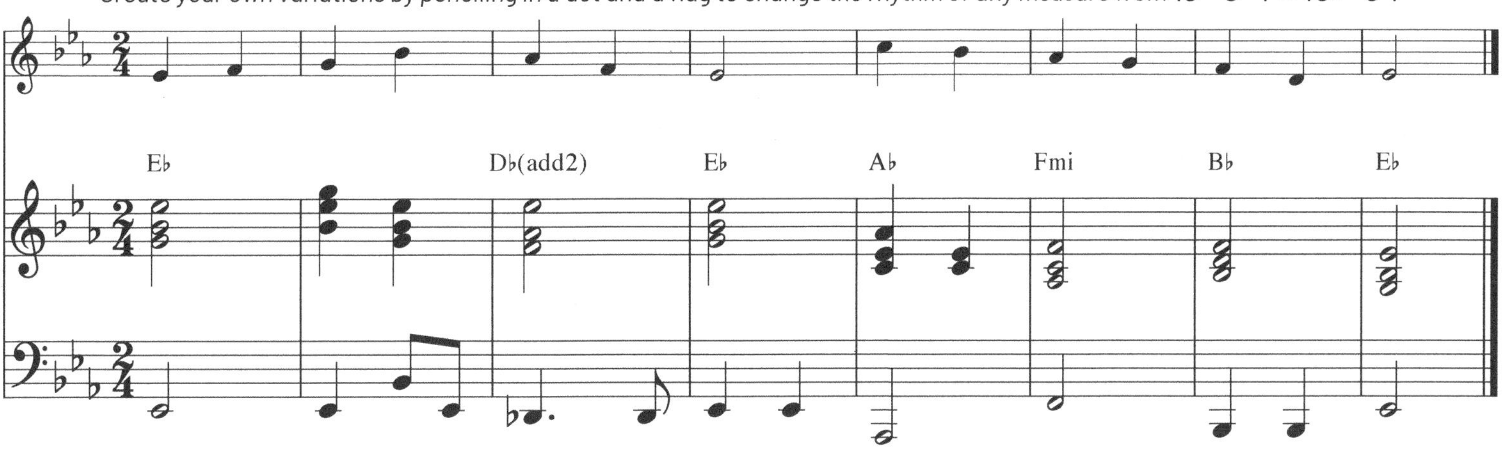

138. EASY GORILLA JUMPS

139. TECHNIQUE TRAX

140. MORE TECHNIQUE TRAX

141. GERMAN FOLK SONG

142. THE SAINTS GO MARCHIN' AGAIN

James Black and Katherine Purvis

143. LOWLAND GORILLA WALK

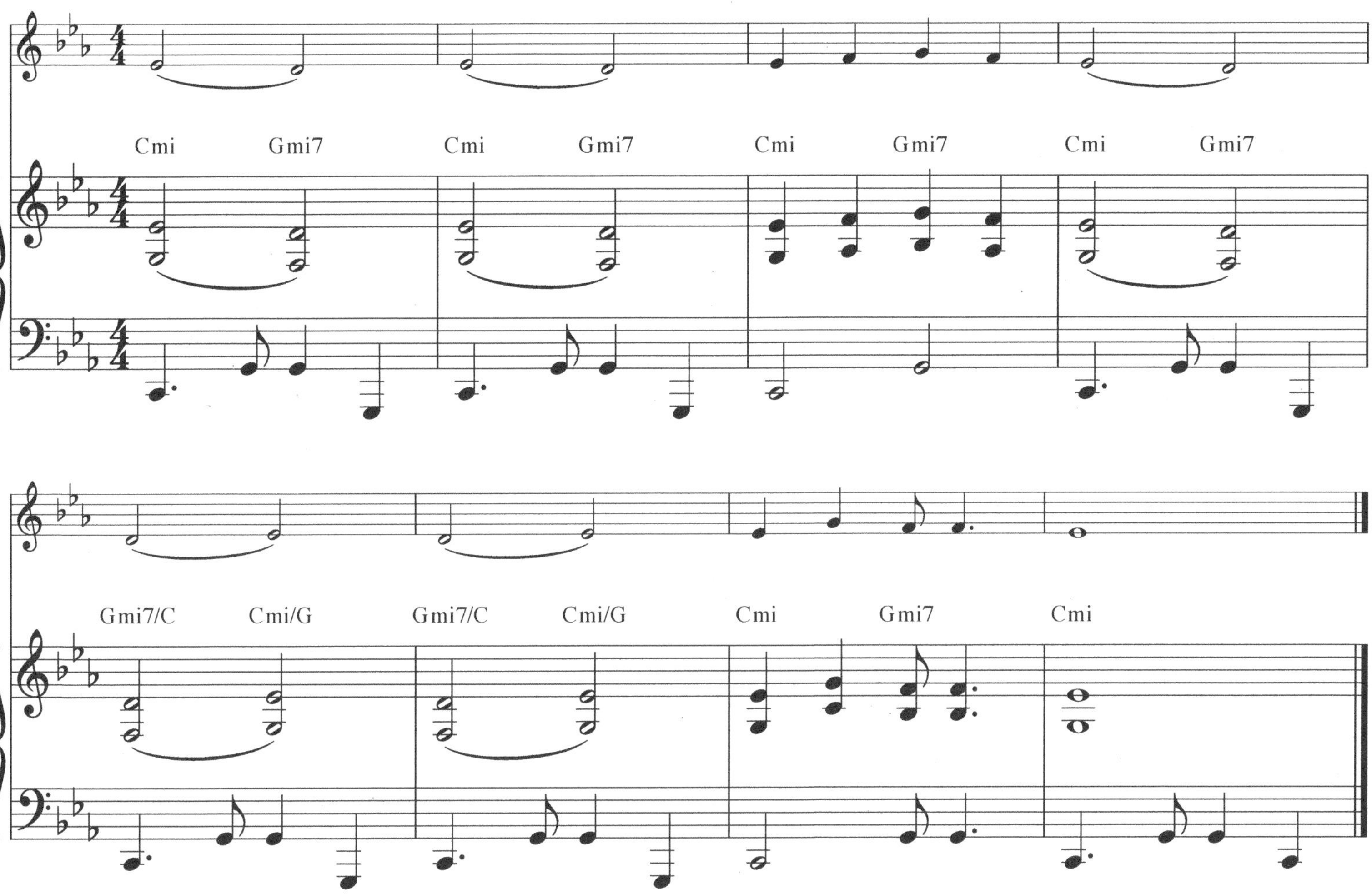

144. SMOOTH SAILING

145. MORE GORILLA JUMPS

146. FULL COVERAGE

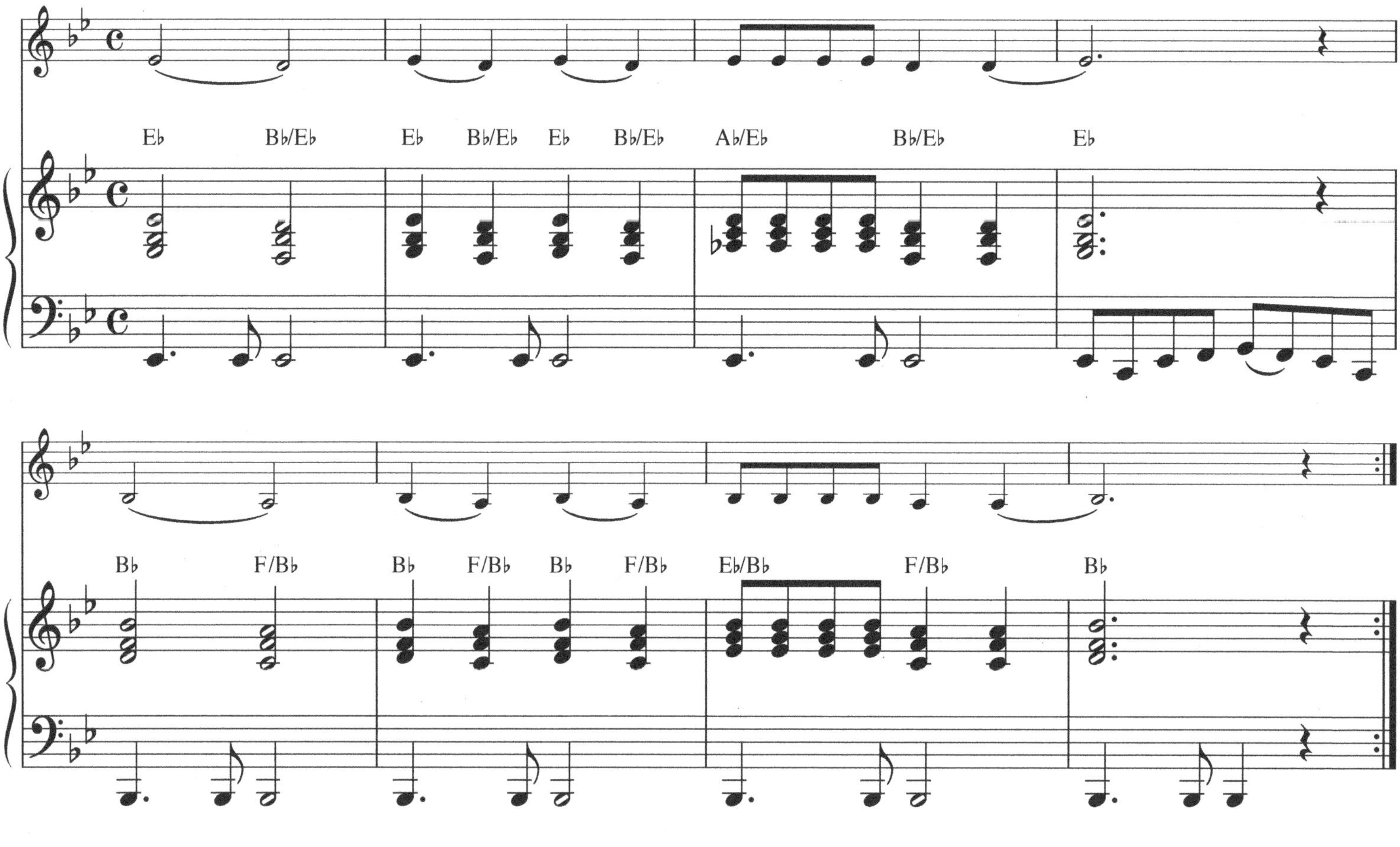

147. CONCERT B♭ SCALE

148. IN HARMONY

149. SCALE AND ARPEGGIO

150. THEME FROM "SURPRISE SYMPHONY"

Franz Josef Haydn

151. ESSENTIAL ELEMENTS QUIZ – THE STREETS OF LAREDO

American Folk Song

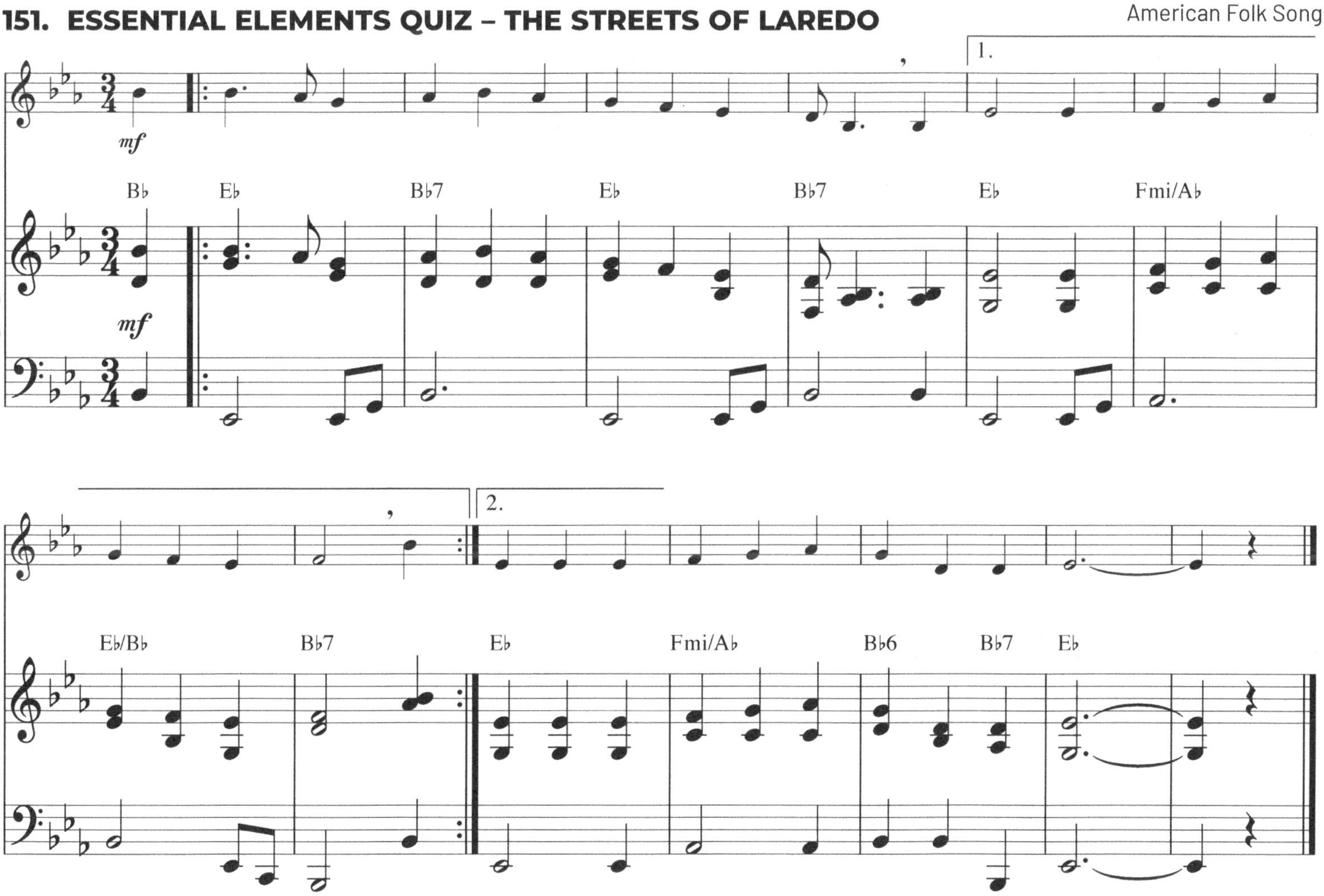

152. SCHOOL SPIRIT – Band Arrangement

W.T. Purdy
Arr. by John Higgins

21
E♭
A♭6
29
f
f
(A♭6)
G
A♭
f
B♭/D
E♭
E♭/G
A♭
1.
2.
E♭/B♭
B♭7
E♭
B♭7
E♭

153. CARNIVAL OF VENICE – Band Arrangement

Julius Benedict
Arr. by John Higgins

29
(B♭)
F7
37
B♭
8va
F7
f
p
45
p
mf
(8va)
B♭
F7
B♭
Cmi7
F7
Cmi7
E♭/F
F7
B♭
E♭
B♭/D
Cmi7
B♭
f

154. RANGE AND FLEXIBILITY BUILDER

155. TECHNIQUE TRAX

156. CHORALE

Johann Sebastian Bach

157. HATIKVAH

Israeli National Anthem

158. RHYTHM RAP

159. EIGHTH NOTE MARCH

160. MINUET

Johann Sebastian Bach

161. RHYTHM RAP

162. EIGHTH NOTES OFF THE BEAT

163. EIGHTH NOTE SCRAMBLE

164. ESSENTIAL ELEMENTS QUIZ

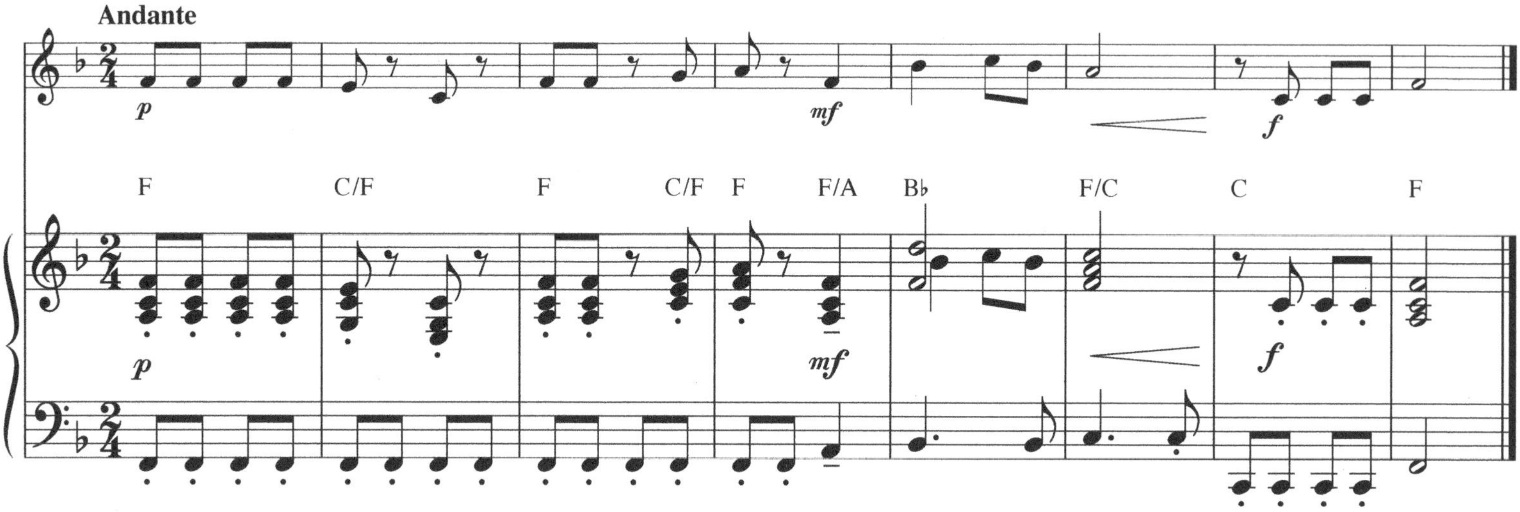

165. DANCING MELODY

166. EL CAPITAN

John Philip Sousa

167. O CANADA

Calixa Lavallee,
l'Hon. Judge Routhier
and Justice R.S. Weir

168. ESSENTIAL ELEMENTS QUIZ – METER MANIA

169. SNAKE CHARMER

170. DARK SHADOWS

171. CLOSE ENCOUNTERS

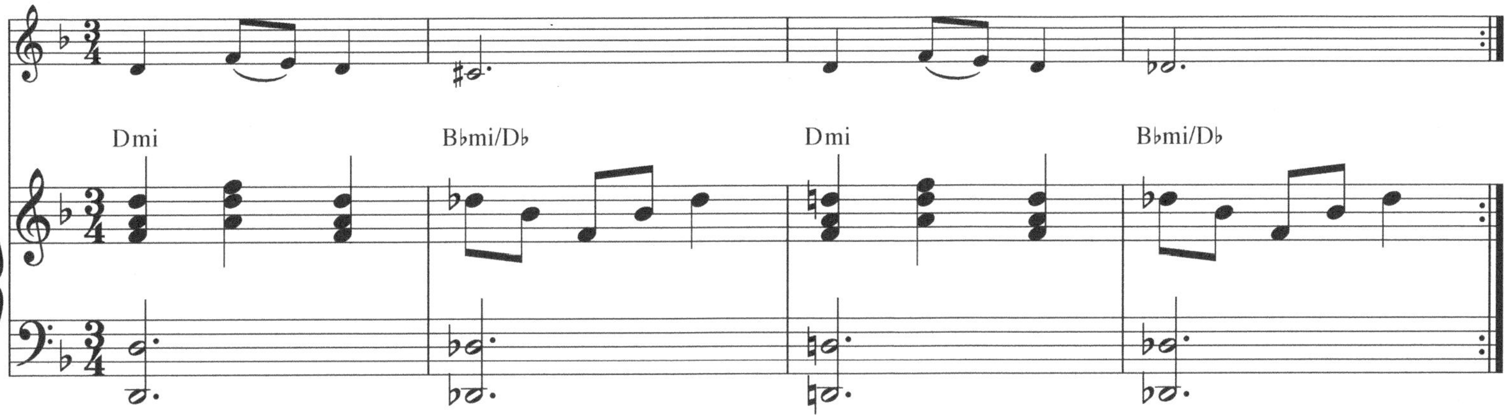

172. MARCH SLAV

Peter Ilyich Tchaikovsky

173. NOTES IN DISGUISE

174. HALF-STEPPIN'

175. EGYPTIAN DANCE

Camille Saint-Saëns

Student Book Page 34

176. SILVER MOON BOAT

Chinese Folk Song

177. THEME FROM SYMPHONY NO. 7 – Duet

Ludwig van Beethoven

B♭mi
D♭/A♭
A♭7
D♭
9
mf
mf
D♭
C
F9
F7
B♭
B♭mi
mf
1.
2.
F/A
B♭mi
F7
B♭mi
F7
B♭mi

178. CAPRICCIO ITALIEN

Peter Ilyich Tchaikovsky

179. AMERICAN PATROL

F.W. Meacham

180. WAYFARING STRANGER

African-American Spiritual

181. ESSENTIAL ELEMENTS QUIZ – SCALE COUNTING CONQUEST

182. AMERICA THE BEAUTIFUL – Band Arrangement

Samuel A. Ward
Arr. by John Higgins

Fmi7 Bb7 Fmi7/C Bb7/D Bb7 Fmi/C Bb7/D Eb Fmi7 Eb/G Eb Ab Eb/G Bb7/F Eb N.C.
mf
25 Maestoso
Bb/D Cmi Cmi/Bb Ab Cmi7/G Fmi7 Eb Bb/D Cmi7 Bb N.C.
f
Bb Eb

183. LA CUCARACHA – Band Arrangement

Latin American Folk Song
Arr. by John Higgins

B♭7
A♭
E♭/G
Fmi
E♭
B♭7
E♭
B♭
B♭7
1.
E♭
2.
B♭7
B♭
A♭/B♭
Gmi/C
B♭7/D
E♭

184. THEME FROM 1812 OVERTURE – Band Arrangement

Peter Ilyich Tchaikovsky
Arr. by John Higgins

Fmi/B♭
E♭/B♭
18
mf
mf
E♭/B♭
B♭
E♭/B♭
Fmi/B♭ C/B♭ Fmi/B♭ C/B♭
mf
p
26
f
f
Fmi/B♭ F7/B♭ B♭
B♭/A♭
E♭/G
B♭
E♭
f

(E♭)
Fmi/E♭
E♭
34
E♭/B♭
Cmi
E♭/B♭
E♭
Fmi/E♭

42
Fmi/D
Fmi/C
E♭/B♭
Cmi
A♭
B♭
G°
Fmi
A° Gmi/B♭ Dmi F7/E♭ N.C.
E♭
B♭
E♭
B♭
E♭
N.C.

185. EINE KLEINE NACHTMUSIK – Solo *(Concert E♭ version: Flute, Alto Sax.)*

Wolfgang Amadeus Mozart
Arr. by John Higgins

185. EINE KLEINE NACHTMUSIK – Solo *(Concert B♭ version: Oboe, Clarinet)*

Wolfgang Amadeus Mozart
Arr. by John Higgins

Student Book Page 38

185. THEME FROM SYMPHONY NO. 1 – Solo

(Concert E♭ version: Bsn., Alto Cl., Bar. Sax., Tpt., Tbn., Bar. B.C., Bar. T.C., Tuba)

Johannes Brahms
Arr. by John Higgins

185. THEME FROM SYMPHONY NO. 1 – Solo *(Concert B♭ version: Bs. Cl., T. Sax., F Horn)*

Johannes Brahms
Arr. by John Higgins

186. SWING LOW, SWEET CHARIOT – Duet

African-American Spiritual

187. LA BAMBA – Duet

Mexican Folk Song

KEY OF CONCERT B♭ MAJOR

1.

2.

3.

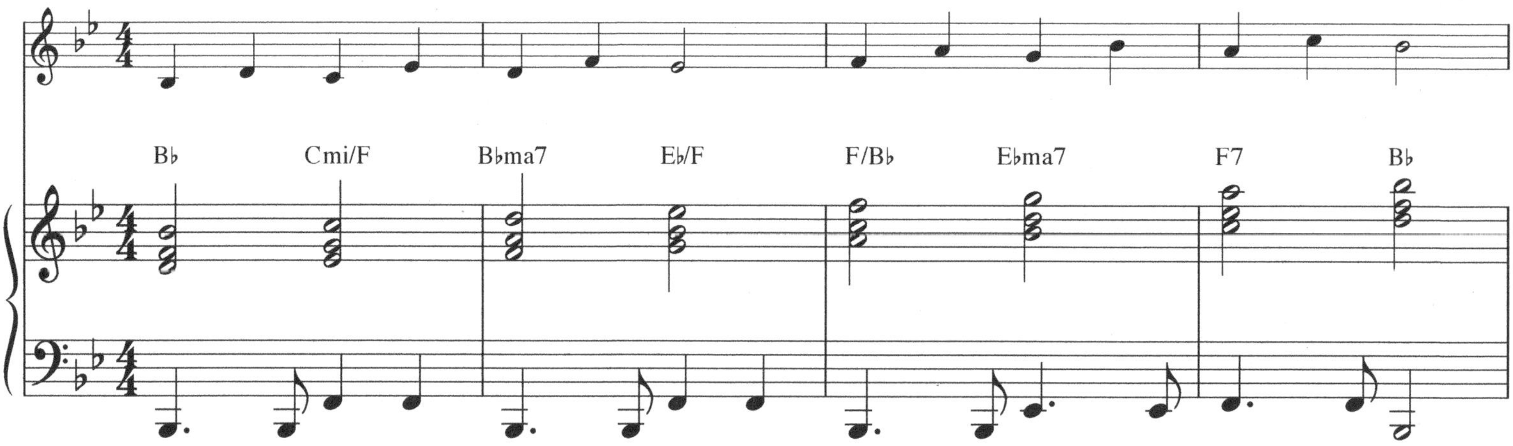

Eb/F
Dmi/F
Eb/F
Dmi/F
Abma7
Bb
F9
Bb

4.

Bb
F
Gmi
Ab
Bb
F
Bb
F
Gmi
Ab
F
Bb
F
Gmi
Ab
Bb
F
Gmi
F
Ebma7
Eb
F
Bb

KEY OF CONCERT E♭ MAJOR

1.

2.

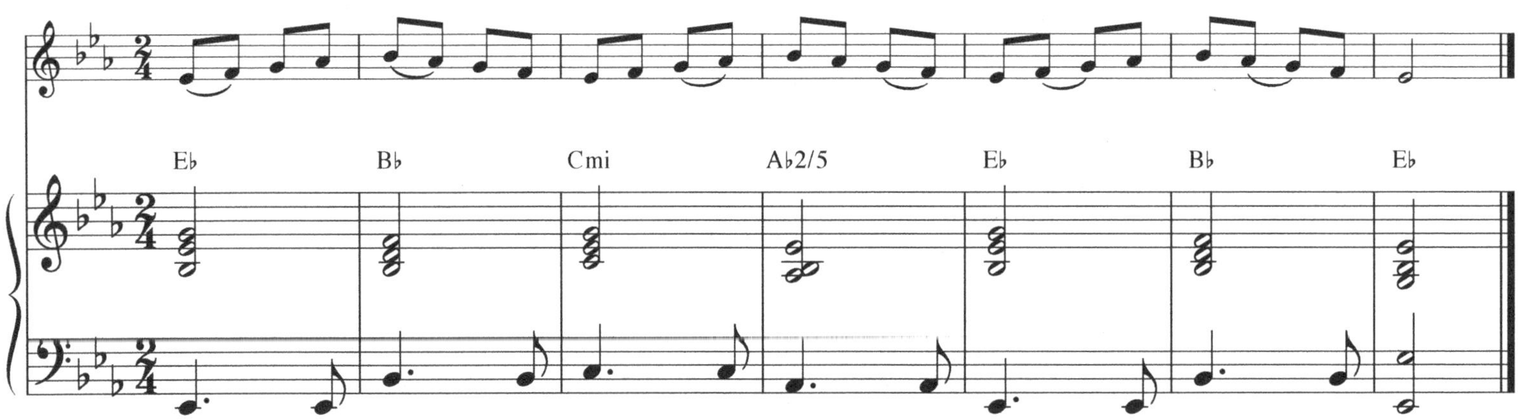

3.

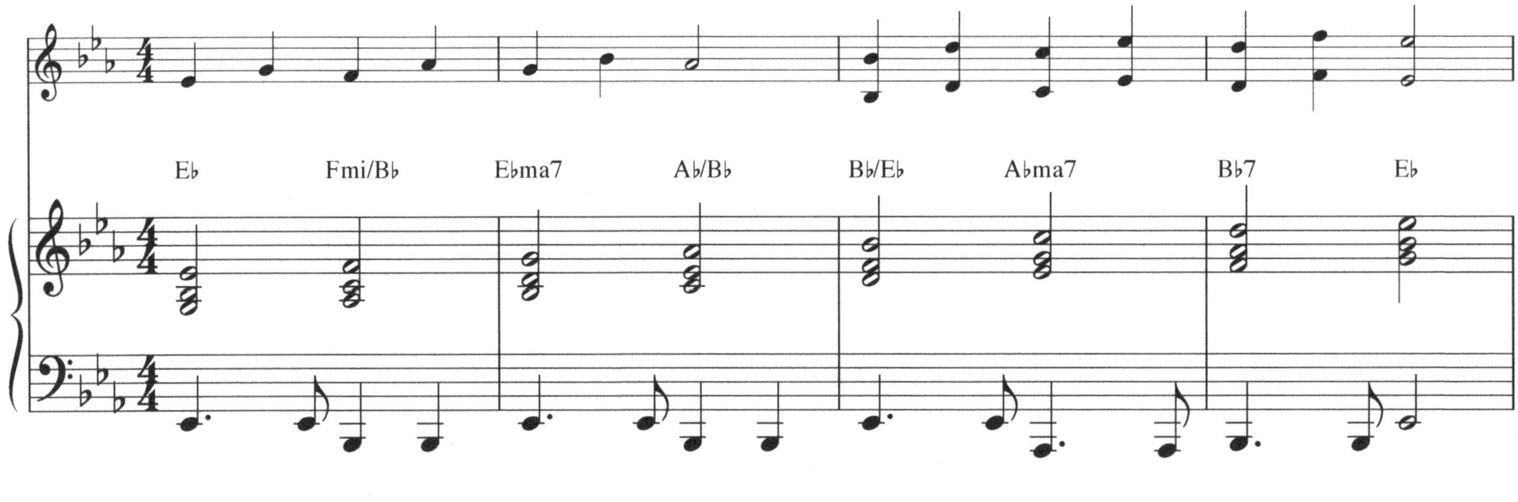

A♭/B♭
Gmi/B♭
A♭/B♭
Gmi/B♭
D♭ma7
E♭
B♭9
E♭

4.

E♭
B♭
Cmi7
D♭
E♭
B♭
E♭
B♭
Cmi7
D♭
B♭
E♭
B♭
Cmi7
D♭
E♭
B♭
Cmi
B♭
A♭ma7
A♭
B♭
E♭

Student Book Page 41

KEY OF CONCERT F MAJOR

1.

2.

3.

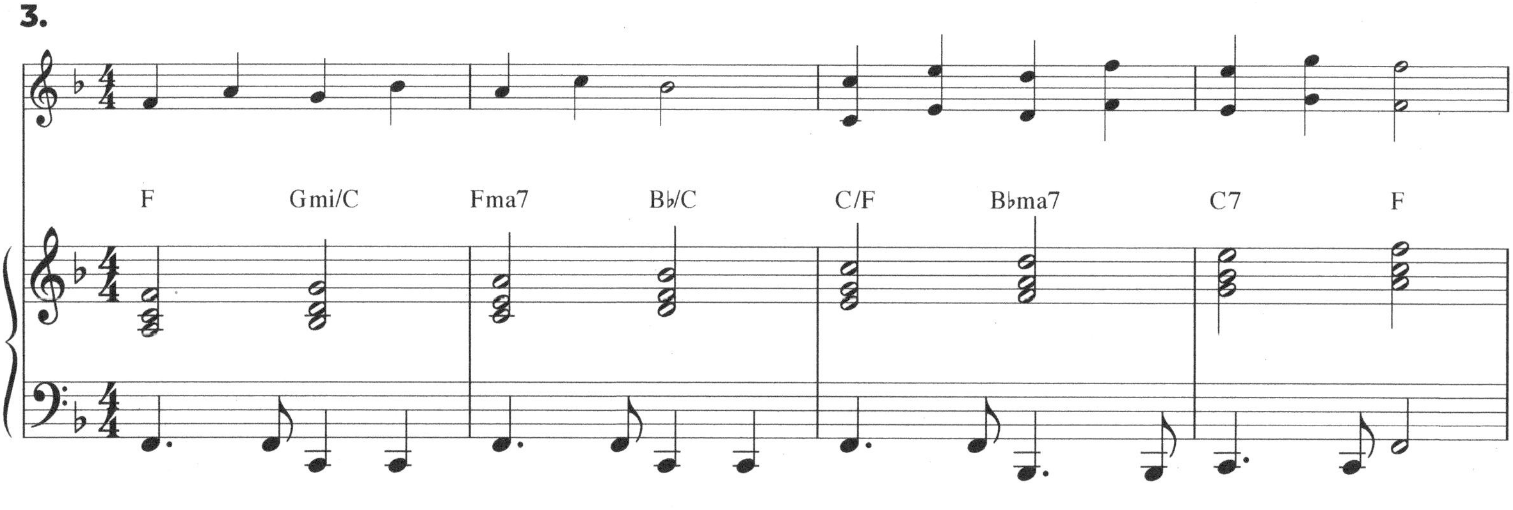

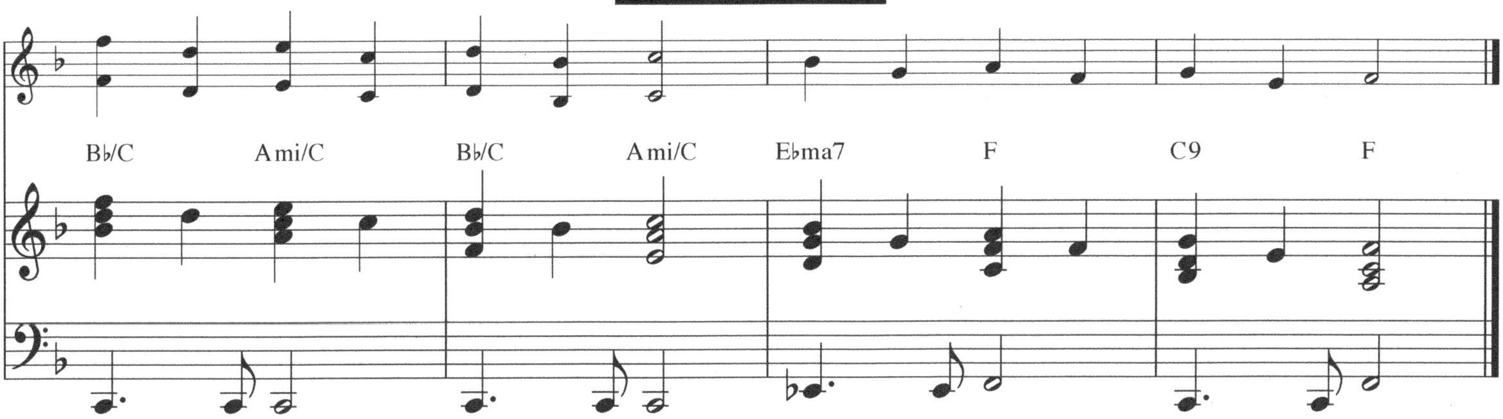
B♭/C
Ami/C
B♭/C
Ami/C
E♭ma7
F
C9
F

4.

F
C
Dmi
E♭
F
C
F
C
Dmi
E♭
C
F
C
Dmi
E♭
F
C
Dmi
C
B♭ma7
B♭
C
F

KEY OF CONCERT A♭ MAJOR

1.

2.

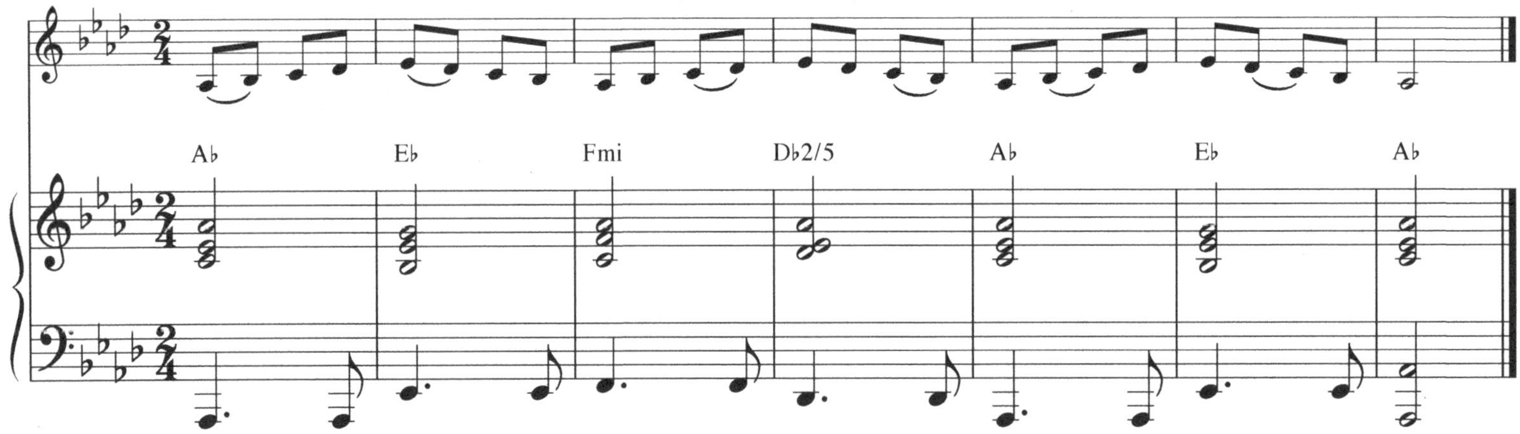

3.

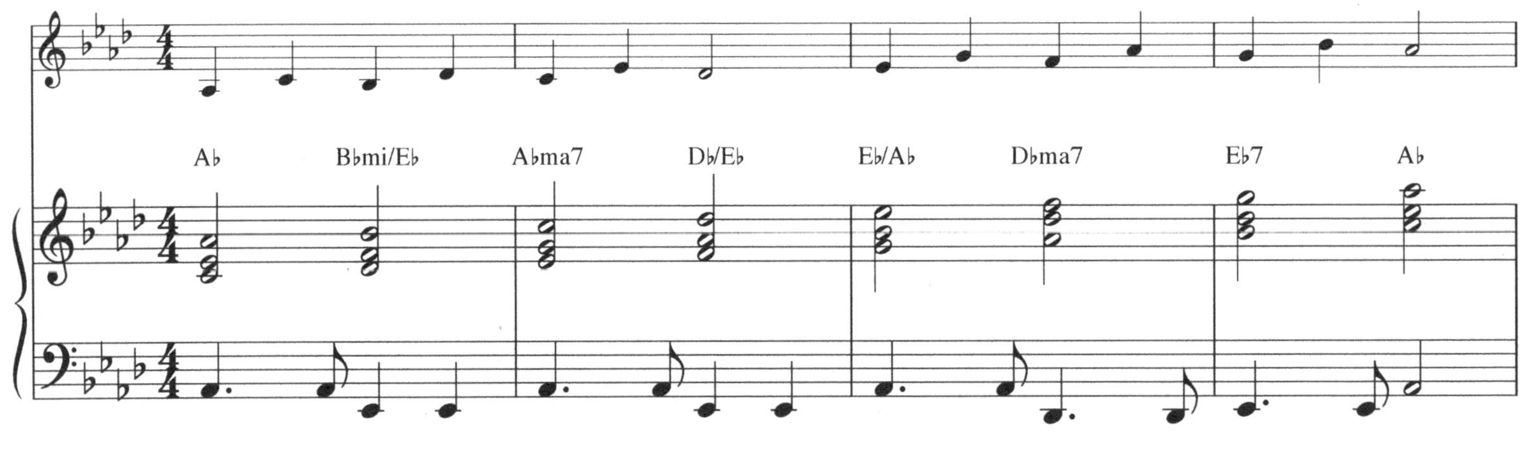

D♭/E♭
C mi/E♭
D♭/E♭
C mi/E♭
G♭ma7
A♭
E♭9
A♭

4.

A♭
E♭
Fmi
G♭
A♭
E♭
A♭
E♭
Fmi
G♭
E♭
A♭
E♭
Fmi
G♭
A♭
E♭
Fmi
E♭
D♭ma7
D♭
E♭
A♭